the Vodka

party book

R&R PUBLICATIONS MARKETING PTY LTD

R&R Publications Marketing Pty Ltd
PO Box 254, Carlton North
Victoria 3054, Australia
Phone (613) 9381 2199
Fax (613) 9381 2689
Email: info@randrpublications.com.au
Website: www.randrpublications.com.au
Australia-wide toll-free: 1800 063 296
© Anthony Carroll 2008

Publisher: Anthony Carroll
Designer: Aisling Gallagher
Photography and Styling: Brent Parker Jones
Food Stylist: Lee Blaylock
Presentation: R&R PhotoStudio
Proofreader: Kate Evans

ISBN: 9-781740-225-37-3

First Printed: May 2006
This Edition: March 2008
Printed in Indonesia

Cover image: Screwdriver page 91

Contents

Introduction   5

Vodka   13

Appetisers   97

Index   128

The History of Vodka

Vodka is a pure, typically colourless spirit, usually distilled from grain or potatoes, however it can also be distilled from many other raw materials. It's charcoal-filtered which removes certain oils and congenerics. The name derives from 'Zhiznennia vodka' = 'Water of Life'. The name Vodka or Wodka means 'Little Water'.

Vodka has no absolute known origin. There are records that point to its use in 1405 in the Sandomierz Court Registry in Poland, but whether it was used as a dry cleaning fluid, a medicine or as a great means of instilling bravery in the hands of the soldiers of the time, we do not know. In Russia the word 'Vodka' was written in an official document and decreed by the Empress Catherine I in the year 1751 and this was to regulate the ownership of Vodka distilleries.

Vodka is believed to have originated in Russia in the grain-growing region that now embraces Belarus, Ukraine and western Russia, however it also has a long tradition in Scandinavia.

It took almost 200 years from 1751 to 1951 for vodka to move outside Europe by way of post-war France, and start to be accepted by the USA. However, by 1975 vodka sales in the United States had outsold any other spirit, the position previously held by bourbon whiskey. It is believed that part of its popularity was its reputation as an alcoholic beverage that leaves no smell of liquor on the breath. The Russians had trademarked vodka, however this went into limbo with the Russian Revolution, when numerous distilleries opened up in the West and sold their own versions of this versatile spirit. A number of court cases followed with the end result being that in 1982 the USSR was granted the right to call vodka the Russian original alcoholic beverage and the court recognised the Soviet trademark motto 'Only vodka from Russia is genuine Russian vodka'.

How Vodka is Made

To make vodka, forget about all of the 'hype' and use of organic vegetables or grains; elaborate filters such as quartz, limestone, charcoal and sand; and the use of pure mountain-stream water and get down to a very simple process. All you need to get started is to make a mash of your favourite grain or vegetable, perhaps potato (which seems to have a reputation when making vodka), and then distil it in a typical continuous still. To make the end product clearer and further reduce any taste, run it through the filter a second or third time; the end result will be milder and smoother.

There is no need to add botanicals during distillation, this is normally done in most other liqueurs to add flavour, but with vodka the secret is to have no taste, so the clearer and cleaner your distillation the better the spirit.

This book is not designed to assist you in making the spirit instead the information provided aims to provide ideas for lots of great vodka cocktails, together with some fabulous appetisers to have at your 'Vodka Party'.

Vodka Infusions

Vodka is ideal for fruit, herb or spice infusions, as the neutral-tasting spirit can easily be mixed to produce some very tasty concoctions.

Select some attractive clear glass bottles with wide mouths. These bottles should hold around 26 oz–32 oz/750–1 ltr of fluid.

Take one of your bottles and place a quantity of any selection of ripe fruit or/and herbs and spices, and push it into the bottle, then fill the bottle with your favourite vodka, the more ingredient you infuse the better the result.

You will find that strong flavours, such as citrus will steep in one to two days while milder flavours will take up to a couple of weeks.

You will find that some ingredients will breakdown during

steep time and will require you to strain the liquid before using. A paper coffee filter is great for use as a liqueur strainer, however a metal strainer can be used but you will find that the end liquid is not as clear as you may like. During the time of infusion store the bottles in the refrigerator as chilling helps to keep the flavours longer.

Step-by-step Infusion Guidelines

1. Pick a good-quality vodka to ensure a good base.

2. Select ingredients to generate the flavour sensation you are hoping to capture. Choose a combination of fresh fruit, spices and herbs.

3. Use a clean, fully sealable glass bottle large enough to contain the vodka and fruit. The bottle must be clean and have a tight seal. The size and nature of the ingredients being infused will dictate the size of the container needed. You can also use the original vodka bottle itself if the ingredients are small enough to fit (i.e. chilli, cinnamon sticks).

4. Insert cut-up pieces of the ingredient into the glass bottle Add secondary flavours (spices, etc) if desired.

5. Reseal the bottle tightly and lay it on its side. Plan to 'steep' the bottle between 24 and 48 hours for most ingredients. Some ingredients may take a week or longer. Ideally the bottle or container is kept in a dark place and should be turned every few hours during the steeping. The timelines are different for every ingredient and depend on how much of the taste transfer you hope to achieve. Be cautious of spices or strong ingredients as a prolonged steeping period could leave you with too much of your desired flavour (i.e. chilli, garlic). If the infusion process has left you with too strong a taste one of the advantages of infusion is that you can simply add more vodka to dilute the taste.

7. After you have removed the flavouring ingredients, the bottle should be sealed and stored in either the fridge or freezer. Depending on the ingredients you may need to use a strainer to properly remove the entire ingredient. Some ingredients can be left in the infused bottle to add a little colour and decoration to the vodka. Examples could include thin fruit slices.

8. If adding numerous ingredients take note of the quantities of each so you can capture the same flavour in the future.

Apple and Cinnamon
4 cinnamon sticks
6 large red apples
750mL bottle of vodka of choice

Slice the apples and toss them into your infusion jar with the cinnamon sticks. Add the bottle of vodka, and let it infuse for a few days. This makes a great hot apple cider cocktail.

Apricot Vodka
1 dozen apricot seeds
750mL bottle of vodka of choice

Place the seeds in a jar and pour in the vodka. Let sit at room temperature for 24 hours. Taste. Strain it or let it sit another 24 hours and taste again.

Blueberry Martini
1 pint blueberries
750mL bottle of vodka of choice
1 cup raspberry liqueur
juice of 1 lime
1 twist of lime zest

Put a small nick in each of the blueberries and put in a glass jar. Pour the vodka over the blueberries then add the raspberry liqueur. Let sit in a dark place for 2 weeks.

Cantaloupe Vodka
5 cups cantaloupe
750mL bottle of vodka of choice

Cut the cantaloupe into large cubes. Toss into your infusion jar and pour the vodka on top. Infuse for about 5 days.

Cherry Vodka

punnet of cherries
750mL bottle of vodka of choice

Pit all the cherries. Remove the stem and place the cherry in the pitter with the indentation facing up. Squeeze the handles together to force out the pit. Then add the cherries and 750mL of vodka into the infusion jar. Infuse for a few days.

Citrus Vodka

15 oranges
10 lemons
1 lime
fresh ginger root, 5cm long
2 cups sugar
750mL bottle of vodka of choice

Cut oranges and lemons into thick rounds. Slice limes thinly. Trim ends and soft spots on ginger root, peel skin and cut into slices. Place half of all fruit and ginger into glass jar, then pour 1 cup sugar evenly over them. Repeat process with remaining fruit, ginger and sugar. Pour vodka over mixture until the jar is full. Infuse for 2–3 days.

Cranberry Spice Vodka

1 cup fresh or frozen cranberries
5 whole cloves
1 whole nutmeg, cracked
1 teaspoon whole coriander seed, cracked
$1/2$ vanilla bean
$1/2$ stick cinnamon, cracked
750mL bottle of vodka of choice

Place cranberries and spices in an infusion jar and top with vodka. Let infuse for 2–3 days, then strain before serving.

Limoncello

10 lemons
750mL bottle of vodka of choice
3 cups white sugar
4 cups water

Zest the lemons, and place into a large jar. Pour vodka over the zest. Cover loosely and let infuse for 1 week at room temperature. After 1 week, combine sugar and water in a medium saucepan. Bring to a boil and boil for 15 minutes, do not stir. Allow syrup to cool to room temperature. Stir vodka mixture into syrup. Strain into glass bottles, and seal each bottle with a cork. Let mixture age for 2 weeks at room temperature. Place bottled liqueur into the freezer. When icy cold, serve in chilled vodka glasses or shot glasses.

Suggested infusion times

Allow 1–3 days for fruits such as lemon, oranges, grapefruits, limes as well as apricots and sliced apples. For herbs such as mint, garlic, tarragon, basic, oregano, dill, thyme, anise, kaffir and lime leaf, infuse just 1–2 days. Infuse 2–3 days for sliced chillies, horseradish, strawberries, pineapples, raspberries, pitted cherries, mangoes, and blueberries. And it may takes as many as 5 days for ingredients such as vanilla bean, fennel, pear, cantaloupe, honeydew, watermelon, coconut, tomatoes, dried fruits, peaches, cucumbers, and ginger.

Pear and Nutmeg Vodka

1 red pear, cut in half
200g dried pears
1 whole nutmeg, cracked in half
750mL bottle of vodka of choice

Rinse fresh pear well. Place fruit and nutmeg in an infusion jar and top with vodka. You can infuse these ingredients but it can be served after 5 days. Strain and place infused vodka in a container.

Pineapple Kiss

2 cups chopped fresh pineapple
2 sprigs fresh mint
750mL bottle of vodka of choice

Place chopped pineapple in glass jar. Add the fresh mint. Pour the vodka over. Infuse for 2–3 days.

Strawberry Vodka

punnet of strawberries
750mL bottle of vodka of choice

Remove the green leafy hull with a paring knife and cut the strawberries in half. Add the strawberries and vodka into the infusion jar and let the strawberries infuse with the vodka for 2–3 days.

Tuscan Vodka

750mL bottle of vodka of choice
1 lemon, quartered or left whole
sprig fresh rosemary
1 large sprig fresh basil

Rinse lemon and herbs well. Place in an infusion jar and top with vodka. Let infuse for 2 days, then strain and place infused vodka in a container.

Blood Hound

Vodkas

Aberfoyle 14	Cape Cod 43	Fools Gold 70
Absolut Wonder 14	Cherry Ripe 43	Fudgesicle 70
Appletini 14	Chi Chi 46	Fuzzy Navel 70
Aqueduct 19	Chocolate Raspberry	Gale at Sea 75
Badgertini 19	Martini 46	Gibson 75
Bay Breeze 19	Chocolatini 46	Godchild 75
Beer Buster 22	Citron Dragon 51	Godmother 78
Bewitched 22	Clamato Cocktail 51	Greyhound 78
Black and Silver 22	Cosmopolitan 51	Harvey Wallbanger 78
Black Eye 27	Cranberry Christmas	Kamikaze 83
Black Magic 27	Punch 54	Kangaroo Cocktail 83
Black Russian 27	Czarine 54	Karoff 83
Blood Hound 30	Deanne 54	Long Island Iced Tea 86
Bloody Mary 30	Deliberation 59	Morning Glory 86
Bluebeard 30	Dessert Shield 59	Moscow Mule 86
Blue Hawaii 35	Dusty Dog 59	Salty Dog 91
Blue Lagoon 35	Electric Lemonade 62	Screwdriver 91
Blue Martini 35	Electric Martini 62	Sex on the Beach 91
Blue Monday 38	Exterminator 62	Vodka Collins 94
Brass Monkey 38	Firefly 67	White Russian 94
Bullfrog 38	Flirtini 67	
Butterscotch Martini 43	Flying Dutchman 67	

Aberfoyle

$1^{1}/_{2}$ oz/45mL vodka
1 oz/30mL Drambuie

Combine ingredients in an old fashioned glass filled with crushed ice. Stir well.

Absolut Wonder

3 oz/90mL Absolut Vanilla Vodka
1 oz/30mL white chocolate liqueur
maraschino cherry to garnish

Combine liquid ingredients in a cocktail shaker with cracked ice. Shake well and strain into a chilled 5 oz/140mL cocktail glass. Garnish with a maraschino cherry.

Appletini

2 oz/60mL vodka
$^{1}/_{2}$ oz/15mL schnapps
$^{1}/_{2}$ oz/15mL apple cider
apple slice to garnish

Combine liquid ingredients in a cocktail shaker with cracked ice. Shake well and strain into a chilled 5 oz/140mL cocktail glass. Garnish with an apple slice.

Aberfoyle

Absolut Wonder

Appletini

Aqueduct

Aqueduct

1½ oz/45mL vodka
1 tsp white curacao
1 tsp apricot brandy
1 tsp lime juice
1 tsp lemon juice
lemon twist

Combine liquid ingredients in a cocktail shaker with cracked ice. Shake well and strain into a chilled 3 oz/90mL martini glass. Garnish with the lemon twist.

Badgertini

1½ oz/45mL vodka
½ oz/15mL sloe gin
¼ oz/15mL lime juice

Combine ingredients in a cocktail shaker with cracked ice. Shake well and strain into a chilled 5 oz/140mL cocktail glass. Can also be served 'straight up' in a rocks glass filled with ice.

Bay Breeze

1½ oz/45mL vodka
3 oz/90mL pineapple juice
1 oz/30mL cranberry juice
pineapple wedge to garnish

Combine liquid ingredients over ice in a highball or Collins glass and stir well. Garnish with pineapple wedge. Serve with swizzle stick and straw.

Badgertini

Bay Breeze

Beer Buster

1$\frac{1}{2}$ oz/45mL vodka
2 dashes Tabasco
12 oz/340mL beer

Stir vodka and tobasco together in a chilled beer mug or pint glass. Pour in beer.

Bewitched

$\frac{1}{2}$ oz/15mL vodka
$\frac{1}{2}$ oz/15mL Benedictine and Brandy
$\frac{1}{2}$ oz/15mL cream

Combine ingredients in a mixing glass with ice. Stir gently and strain into a large shot glass or cordial glass.

Black and Silver

2 oz/60mL vodka
$\frac{1}{2}$ oz/15mL Chambord

Combine ingredients in a cocktail shaker with cracked ice and shake well. Pour into a chilled 3 oz/90mL martini glass.

Beer Buster

Bewitched

Black and Silver

Black Eye

Black Eye

1½ oz/45mL vodka
½ oz/15mL blackberry brandy

Combine ingredients in a mixing glass filled with crushed ice. Stir well and strain into a 5 oz/140mL cocktail glass.

Black Magic

1½ oz/45mL vodka
½ oz/15mL black sambuca

Combine ingredients in a mixing glass filled with crushed ice. Stir well and strain into a 5 oz/140mL cocktail glass.

Black Russian

2 oz/60mL vodka
1 oz/30mL Kahlua

Combine ingredients in an old-fashioned glass filled with crushed ice. Stir.

Black Magic

Black Russian

Blood Hound

1½ oz/45mL vodka
1 dash sweet vermouth
1 dash dry vermouth
strawberry to garnish

Combine in a mixing glass with ice. Swirl the ingredients gently and strain into a chilled 5oz/140mL cocktail glass. Garnish with a fresh strawberry.

Bloody Mary

1½ oz/45mL vodka
1½ tsps lemon juice
2 drops Worcestershire
2 drops Tabasco
salt and pepper to taste
tomato juice
celery stick to garnish

Combine liquid ingredients over ice in a highball or Collins glass and stir well. Garnish with celery stick, olive, marinated string bean or vegetable of choice. Serve with swizzle stick and straw.

Bluebeard

1½ oz/45mL vodka
½ oz/15mL blueberry brandy

Combine ingredients in a mixing glass filled with crushed ice. Stir well and strain into a 5 oz/140mL cocktail glass.

Blood Hound

Bloody Mary

Bluebeard

Blue Hawaii

Blue Hawaii

1½ oz/45mL vodka
½ oz/15mL blue curacao
1½ tsps crème de coconut
4 oz/125mL pineapple juice

On the Rocks – Combine ingredients in a shaker with ice. Mix well and strain into a Collins or small hurricane glass filled with crushed ice. **Blended** – Combine ingredients with a scoop of ice in an electric blender. Mix well (15–20 seconds). Pour into Collins or small hurricane glass.

Blue Lagoon

1½ oz/45mL vodka
½ oz/15mL blue curacao
4 oz/125mL lemonade
maraschino cherry
orange slice

Combine liquid ingredients in a Collins or highball glass filled with ice cubes. Stir well. Garnish with the cherry and orange slice.

Blue Martini

1½ oz/45mL vodka   ½ oz/15mL blue curacao
1½ oz/45mL gin   orange twist

Blues Straight Up – Combine liquid ingredients in a cocktail shaker with cracked ice and shake well. Pour into a chilled 5 oz/140mL cocktail glass and serve with a twist of orange. **Blues On the Rocks** – Combine liquid ingredients in a cocktail shaker, stir, pour into a rocks glass filled with ice and serve with a twist of orange.

Blue Lagoon

Blue Martini

Blue Monday

1 oz/30mL vodka
½ oz/15mL Cointreau
½ oz/15mL blue curacao

Combine ingredients in a mixing glass filled with ice cubes. Stir well
and strain into a 3 oz/90mL martini glass.

Brass Monkey

1 oz/30mL vodka
½ oz/15mL light rum
4 oz/125mL orange juice
½ oz/15mL Galliano

Combine the vodka, rum and orange juice into an old-fashioned glass
filled with ice and stir well. Pour the Galliano over the back of
a teaspoon into the glass so that the Galliano floats on top.

Bullfrog

1½ oz/45mL vodka
½ oz/15mL triple sec
6 oz/170mL lemonade or limeade
slice of lemon or lime to garnish

Pour the vodka, triple sec and lemonade or limeade into a Collins glass
filled with ice and stir well. Garnish with a lemon or lime slice.

Blue Monday

Brass Monkey

Bullfrog

Butterscotch Martini

Butterscotch Martini

1½ oz/45mL vodka
½ oz/15mL butterscotch scnapps
½ oz/15mL butterscotch cream liqueur

Combine ingredients in a mixing glass with ice. Swirl gently and strain into a chilled cocktail glass.

Cape Cod

1 oz/30mL vodka
cranberry juice
lime wedge

Add the vodka to a highball glass filled with ice, then top-up with cranberry juice. Squeeze lime wedge into glass and drop it in.

Cherry Ripe

1½ oz/45mL vodka
½ oz/15mL cherry brandy
½ oz/15mL brandy
maraschino cherry

Combine liquid ingredients in a mixing glass filled with ice cubes. Stir well and strain into a 3 oz/90mL martini glass and garnish with the cherry.

Cape Cod

Cherry Ripe

Chi Chi

1½ oz/45mL vodka   ½ banana
2 oz/60mL pineapple juice   pineapple wedge to garnish
1 oz/30mL crème de coconut

Combine vodka, pineapple juice, crème de coconut and banana in an
electric blender with crushed ice. Blend 20–30 seconds. Pour blended
mixture into a Collins glass. Garnish with wedge of pineapple and
umbrella.

Chocolate Raspberry Martini

1½ oz/45mL vodka
½ oz/15mL Godiva chocolate liqueur
splash of soda
raspberry to garnish

Combine vodka and chocolate liquer ingredients in a cocktail shaker
with cracked ice. Shake well and strain into a chilled 3 oz/90mL martini
glass. Top with a splash of soda. Garnish with a fresh raspberry.

Chocolatini

2 oz/60mL vodka
1 oz/30mL Godiva chocolate liqueur
cocoa powder
chocolate flake

Wet rim of a 3 oz/90mL martini glass and dip into cocoa powder.
Combine vodka and chocolate liqueur in a cocktail shaker with ice.
Shake well to chill. Then strain into the martini glass. Use a chocolate
flake for garnish.

Chi Chi

Chocolate Raspberry Martini

Chocolatini

Citron Dragon

Citron Dragon

1$\frac{1}{2}$ oz/45mL Absolut Citron Vodka
$\frac{1}{2}$ oz/15mL Cointreau
1 oz/30mL melon liqueur
splash of soda
lemon twist to garnish

Combine liquid ingredients in a cocktail shaker with cracked ice and shake well. Pour into a chilled 5 oz/140mL cocktail glass. Garnish with a lemon twist.

Clamato Cocktail

2$\frac{1}{2}$ oz/75mL vodka
3 oz/90mL tomato juice
sprinkle of black pepper

dash Worcestershire sauce
dash Tobasco sauce
lemon wedge

Combine liquid ingredients in a cocktail shaker with cracked ice, add black pepper and shake well. Strain into a chilled Collins or highball glass. Garnish with a lemon wedge.

Cosmopolitan

1$\frac{1}{2}$ oz/45mL vodka
$\frac{1}{2}$ oz/15mL Cointreau
$\frac{3}{4}$ oz/22mL cranberry juice
1$\frac{1}{2}$ tsps lime juice
lime twist to garnish

Combine liquid ingredients in a cocktail shaker with cracked ice and shake well. Pour into a chilled 5 oz/140mL cocktail glass. Garnish with a lime twist.

Clamato Cocktail

Cosmopolitan

Cranberry Christmas Punch

2 cups vodka
4 cups cranberry juice
1½ cups Rose's lime cordial
2 cups water
3 tbsp sugar

Combine all ingredients in a large punch bowl. Add a large block of ice to keep it all cool. Serves 20.

Czarine

1 oz/30mL vodka
½ oz/15mL dry vermouth
½ oz/15mL apricot brandy
dash bitters

Combine ingredients in a mixing glass filled with ice cubes. Stir well and strain into a 3 oz/90mL martini glass.

Deanne

1 oz/30mL vodka
½ oz/15mL sweet vermouth
½ oz/15mL Cointreau
lemon twist

Combine liquid ingredients in a mixing glass filled with ice cubes. Stir well and strain into a 3 oz/90mL martini glass and garnish with the lemon twist.

Cranberry Christmas Punch

Czarine

Deanne

Deliberation

Deliberation

1½ oz/45mL vodka
½ oz/15mL melon liqueur
lemon and lime twist to garnish

Combine ingredients in a mixing glass filled with ice cubes. Stir well and strain into a 3 oz/90mL martini glass and garnish lemon and lime twist.

Dessert Shield

1½ oz/45mL vodka
½ oz/15mL cranberry liqueur
4 oz/125mL cranberry juice

Combine ingredients in a Collins or highball glass filled with ice cubes. Stir well.

Dusty Dog

2 oz/60mL vodka
½ oz/15mL crème de cassis
1 tsp lemon juice
dash bitters
5 oz/140mL ginger ale
lemon twist

Combine liquid ingredients in a cocktail shaker with cracked ice. Shake well and strain into a chilled highball glass almost filled with clean ice cubes. Garnish with the lemon twist.

Dessert Shield

Dusty Dog

Electric Lemonade

1$\frac{1}{2}$ oz/45mL vodka
$\frac{1}{2}$ oz/15mL blue curacao
2 oz/60mL sweet-and-sour mix
7Up or sprite
lemon slice
maraschino cherry

Combine all the liquid ingredients in a blender and blend for 15–20 seconds until smooth. Pour into a highball glass filled with ice. Garnish with a lemon slice and maraschino cherry.

Electric Martini

2 oz/60mL vodka
$\frac{1}{2}$ oz/15mL blue curacao
$\frac{1}{2}$ oz/15mL sweet-and-sour mix
maraschino cherry to garnish

Combine liquid ingredients in a cocktail shaker with cracked ice. Shake well and strain into a chilled 3 oz/90mL martini glass. Garnish with a maraschino cherry.

Exterminator

2$\frac{1}{2}$ oz/75mL vodka
$\frac{1}{2}$ oz/15mL fino sherry

Combine ingredients in a mixing glass filled with ice cubes. Stir well and strain into a 3 oz/90mL martini glass.

Electric Lemonade

Electric Martini

Exterminator

Firefly

Firefly

1½ oz/45mL vodka
2 oz/60mL grapefruit juice
dash of grenadine
maraschino cherry to garnish

Combine the vodka and grapefruit juice in a Collins glass filled with ice, add grenadine and stir. Garnish with cherry.

Flirtini

1 oz/30mL vodka
2 oz/60mL champagne
2 oz/60mL pineapple juice
pineapple wedge to garnish

Combine all ingredients in a highball or Collins glass filled with ice, stir and serve, garnished with pineapple wedge.

Flying Dutchman

2 oz/60mL vodka
½ oz/15mL green crème de menthe
½ oz/15mL white crème de menthe
lime wedge to garnish

Combine all liquid ingredients in a highball or Collins glass filled with ice, stir and serve, garnished with lime wedge.

Flirtini

Flying Dutchman

Fools Gold

½ oz/15mL vodka
½ oz/15mL Galliano

Combine the ingredients in a shaker filled with ice, shake and strain into a shot glass.

Fudgesicle

1 oz/30mL vodka
1½ tsps crème de cacao
1½ oz/45mL chocolate syrup

Combine the ingredients in a shaker filled with ice, shake and serve in an old-fashioned glass filled with ice.

Fuzzy Navel

1 oz/30mL vodka
1 oz/30mL peach-tree schnapps
4 oz/125mL orange juice
orange slice to garnish

Combine liquid ingredients in a Collins or highball glass filled with ice cubes. Stir well. Garnish with orange slice.

Fools Gold

Fudgesicle

Fuzzy Navel

Gale at Sea

Gale at Sea

1½ oz/45mL vodka
½ oz/15mL dry vermouth
½ oz/15mL Galliano
½ oz/15mL blue curacao

Combine ingredients in a mixing glass filled with ice cubes. Stir well and strain into a 5 oz/140mL cocktail glass.

Gibson

2 oz/60mL vodka
2 drops dry vermouth
cocktail onion to garnish

Combine liquid ingredients in a cocktail shaker with cracked ice and shake well. Pour into a chilled 3 oz/90mL martini glass. Garnish with a cocktail onion.

Godchild

1 oz/30mL vodka
1 oz/30mL amaretto
1 oz/30mL cream
cocktail onion to garnish

Combine liquid ingredients in a cocktail shaker with cracked ice and shake well. Pour into a chilled 3 oz/90mL martini glass. Garnish with a cocktail onion.

Gibson

Godchild

Godmother

1½ oz/45mL vodka
½ oz/15mL amaretto

Combine in an old-fashioned glass with ice.

Greyhound

1 oz/30mL vodka
grapefriut juice
lemon twist to garnish

Combine ingredients in a highball or Collins glass filled with ice, stir and serve, garnished with lemon twist.

Harvey Wallbanger

1½oz/45mL vodka
4 oz/125mL orange juice
½ oz/15mL Galliano
orange slice to garnish

Combine vodka and orange juice in a highball or Collins glass filled with ice and stir well. Float the Galliano on top. Garnish with an orange slice.

Godmother

Greyhound

Harvey Wallbanger

Kamikaze

Kamikaze

1½ oz/45mL vodka
½ oz/15mL Cointreau
2 tsps Rose's lime cordial

Combine ingredients in a mixing glass filled with ice cubes. Stir well and strain into a 5 oz/140mL cocktail glass.

Kangaroo Cocktail

2 oz/60mL vodka
1 oz/30mL dry vermouth
lemon twist

Combine liquid ingredients in a mixing glass filled with ice cubes. Stir well and strain into a 5 oz/140mL cocktail glass. Garnish with lemon twist.

Karoff

1½ oz/45mL vodka
1 oz/30mL cranberry juice
5 oz/140mL club soda
lime wedge

Combine all liquid ingredients in a highball or Collins glass filled with ice and stir well. Garnish with the lime wedge.

Kangaroo Cocktail

Long Island Iced Tea

1 oz/30mL vodka
1 oz/30mL gin
1 oz/30mL light rum
1 oz/30mL tequila

1 oz/30mL lemon juice
1 tsp caster sugar
4 oz/125mL cola
lemon slice

Combine liquid ingredients except the cola in a cocktail shaker with cracked ice. Shake well and strain into a highball or Collins glass almost filled with clean ice cubes. Add the cola and stir well. Garnish with a lemon slice.

Morning Glory

$1\frac{1}{2}$ oz/45mL vodka
$\frac{1}{2}$ oz/15mL dark crème de cacao
2 oz/60mL light cream
$\frac{1}{4}$ tsp grated nutmeg

Combine liquid ingredients in a cocktail shaker with cracked ice. Shake well and strain into a Collins or highball glass almost filled with clean ice cubes. Garnish with the nutmeg.

Moscow Mule

$1\frac{1}{2}$ oz/45mL vodka
1 oz/30mL lime juice
4 oz/125mL ginger beer
lime wedge

Combine all liquid ingredients in a highball or Collins glass filled with clean ice cubes and stir well. Garnish with the lime wedge.

Long Island Iced Tea

Morning Glory

Moscow Mule

Salty Dog

Salty Dog

2 tsps salt   2 oz/60mL vodka
lime wedge   5 oz/140mL grapefruit juice

Place the salt in a saucer. Rub the lime wedge around the rim of a highball, then dip the glass into the salt to coat the rim. Almost fill the glass with ice cubes and pour the vodka and grapefruit juice into the glass. Stir well.

Screwdriver

$1\frac{1}{2}$ oz/45mL vodka
$1\frac{1}{2}$ oz/45mL orange juice

Combine ingredients in an old-fashioned spirit glass filled with clean ice cubes and stir well. A **Comfortable Screw** is made with 1 oz/ 30mL Vodka, $\frac{1}{2}$ oz/15mL Southern Comfort and topped with orange juice. A **Slow Comfortable Screw** has the above ingredients plus the addition of $\frac{1}{2}$ oz/15mL sloe gin. A **Long Slow Comfortable Screw** is a longer drink served in a Collins or highball glass. A **Long Slow Comfortable Screw Up Against A Wall** has all of the above plus the addition of $\frac{1}{2}$ oz/15mL Galliano.

Sex on the Beach

1 oz/30mL vodka   2 oz/60mL cranberry juice
1 oz/30mL peach schnapps   orange slice
2 oz/60mL orange juice

Combine all liquid ingredients in a highball or Collins glass filled with clean ice cubes and stir well. Garnish with the orange slice.

Screwdriver

Sex on the Beach

Vodka Collins

2 oz/60mL vodka
1 oz/30mL lemon juice
1 tsp caster sugar
3 oz/90mL club soda
maraschino cherry
orange slice

Combine first three ingredients in a cocktail shaker with cracked ice. Shake well and strain into a Collins or highball glass almost filled with clean ice cubes. Add the club soda and stir. Garnish with the cherry and orange slice.

White Russian

1½ oz/45mL vodka
1 oz/30mL Kahlua
1 oz/30mL light cream

Combine ingredients in a cocktail shaker with cracked ice. Shake well and strain into an old-fashioned glass almost filled with clean ice cubes.

Vodka Collins

White Russian

Party Appetisers

Pork Frickadellas **98**

Bloody Mary Oyster Shots **101**

Sausage Crostini with Sauerkraut **102**

Herb Blinis with Salmon Roe **105**

Smoked Salmon Canapés **106**

Salami and Cheese Pumpernickel Squares **109**

Marinated Stuffed Mushrooms **110**

Smoked Fish and Egg Turnovers **113**

Leek, Fetta and Sun-dried Tomato Quiches **114**

Mini Lamb Shashlyh **116**

Mini Chicken and Mushroom Pies **119**

Beef and Sauerkraut Triangles **120**

Chicken Drumettes **123**

Pork Frickadellas

1 onion, roughly chopped
1 lb/500g pork mince
2 eggs, lightly beaten
¼ cup plain flour
¼ cup milk
salt and freshly ground black pepper
2 tbsps olive oil
2 tbsp butter
½ cup chunky tomato pasta sauce

Place onion in a food processor. Process onion until finely chopped
Combine onion, pork mince, eggs, flour, milk, salt and pepper in a
bowl (mixture should be quite sloppy). Using wet fingers form mixture
into small meat balls. Place on a baking tray lined with baking paper.
Heat olive oil and butter in a large heavy nonstick frying pan over
low heat. Add meat balls and flatten with a spatula. Cook for about 8
minutes or until cooked, turning from time to time. Serve frickadellas
with tomato pasta sauce. Makes about 30.

Pork Frickadellas

Bloody Mary Oyster Shots

Bloody Mary ✩ Oyster Shots

12 oz / 350mL tomato juice
3¼ oz / 100mL vodka
2 tbsps lemon juice
1 tsp Worcestershire sauce
5–6 drops Tabasco
24 fresh oysters
1 Lebanese cucumber, cut into thin sticks
salt and freshly ground black pepper

Combine tomato juice, vodka, lemon juice, Worcestershire sauce and Tabasco in a large jug. Pour mixture evenly between shot glasses. Place an oyster and a piece of cucumber in each glass and season with salt and pepper. Makes 24.

Sausage Crostini with Sauerkraut

1 french bread stick or baguette, cut into $^3/_4$ in/$1^1/_2$cm slices
olive oil spray
4 Kransky sausages
$^1/_4$ cup mild English mustard
$^2/_3$ cup sauerkraut
salt and freshly ground black pepper

Preheat oven to 430°F/220°C. Place bread slices on a baking tray and spray with olive oil. Place in the oven and cook for 5–6 minutes or until just golden. Place sausages in a saucepan, cover with water. Bring to the boil, and simmer over low heat for 5 minutes or until cooked. Cut each sausage into 14 thin slices. Spread bread evenly with mustard, top with 2 slices of sausage and garnish with sauerkraut. Season with salt and pepper, and serve. Makes about 28.

Sausage Crostini with Sauerkraut

Herb Blinis with Salmon Roe

Herb Blinis with Salmon Roe

1 cup self-raising flour, sifted
1 egg, lightly beaten
¾ cup milk
1 tbsp finely chopped dill
2 tsps thinly sliced chives
salt and freshly ground black pepper
butter for cooking
⅔ cup light sour cream
½ tsp finely grated lemon rind
2 oz/60g jar salmon roe

Combine flour, egg, milk, dill, chives, salt and pepper in a mixing bowl. Whisk together until smooth. Heat a little butter in a nonstick frying pan. Add spoonfuls of mixture in batches (about 2 in/5cm in diameter). Cook for 1–2 minutes each side or until golden. Combine sour cream and lemon rind in a small bowl. Top blinis with a dollop of sour cream and a little salmon roe. Makes about 24.

Smoked Salmon Canapés

⅓ cup light cream cheese
1 tbsp horseradish cream
1 tbsp thinly sliced chives
6 slices rye bread, cut into quarters (Bergen brand)
7 oz/200g smoked salmon, sliced
baby capers to garnish

Combine cream cheese, horseradish cream and chives in a small bowl. Spread bread evenly with cream cheese mixture. Top with smoked salmon and garnish with capers. Makes 24.

Smoked Salmon Canapés

Salami and Cheese Pumpernickel Squares

Salami and Cheese Pumpernickel Squares

½ cup light cream cheese
2 tsps finely chopped continental parsley
2 tsps thinly sliced chives
salt and freshly ground black pepper
24 pumpernickel squares
12 slices salami, halved and thinly sliced
12 sun-dried tomatoes, thinly sliced
chives to garnish

Combine cream cheese, parsley, chives, salt and pepper in a small bowl.
Spread pumpernickel evenly with cream cheese mixture and top with
sliced salami and sundried tomatoes. Garnish with sliced chives.
Makes 24

Marinated Stuffed Mushrooms

When purchasing mushrooms make sure you choose really fresh mushrooms which are firm and white in colour. The older the mushroom the more lemon juice it absorbs, which overpowers the dish.

24 button mushrooms
2 tbsps olive oil
⅓ cup lemon juice
3 hardboiled eggs, mashed
2 tbsps sour cream
1 tbsps sliced chives
salt and freshly ground black pepper
red or black caviar, to garnish

Brush dirt from mushrooms and remove stalks. Combine oil and lemon juice in a bowl. Add mushrooms and toss well. Leave to marinate for about 3 hours or until softened a little. Drain mushrooms and wipe with a paper towel so the mushrooms are not slippery and greasy. Combine eggs, sour cream, chives, salt and pepper in a bowl. Fill mushroom cavities with egg mixture and top with a little caviar. Makes 24.

Marinated Stuffed Mushrooms

Smoked Fish and Egg Turnovers

Smoked Fish and Egg Turnovers

These turnovers are also great using shortcrust pastry.

5 oz/150g smoked ocean trout portion, skin removed and flaked
2 hardboiled eggs, chopped
½ cup cooked long-grain rice
1 tbsp chopped dill
2 tbsps finely chopped dill pickle
2 shallots (green onions), sliced
salt and freshly ground black pepper
6 sheets puff pastry, thawed
1 egg, lightly beaten

Preheat oven to 430°F/220°C. Line a baking tray with baking paper.
Combine fish, hardboiled eggs, rice, dill, dill pickle, shallots, salt and
pepper in a bowl. Cut puff pastry into 4 in/10cm rounds. Place a
heaped tablespoon of mixture in the centre. Brush the edges with
water and press together. Pinch the edges together and place upright
on prepared baking tray. Brush pastries with beaten egg and bake in
the oven for about 15 minutes or until golden and puffed.
Makes about 24.

Leek, Fetta and Sun-dried Tomato Quiches

olive oil spray
1 tbsp olive oil
1 leek, trimmed, halved and sliced
4 eggs, lightly beaten
$\frac{1}{2}$ cup cream
2 tbsps milk
1 tbsp freshly chopped continental parsley
freshly ground black pepper
3 sheets puff pastry, thawed
6–8 sun-dried tomatoes, thinly sliced
2 oz/60g danish fetta cheese, crumbled

Preheat oven to 400°F/200°C. Lightly grease 2 x 12 tart or patty cases
(2 in/6cm in diameter) with olive spray. Heat olive oil in a fry pan.
Cook leeks for 2–3 minutes or until soft. Combine eggs, cream, milk,
parsley and pepper in a jug. Cut pastry into 2¾ in/7cm rounds and line
tart cases with pastry. Divide leek, sun-dried tomatoes and fetta evenly
between pastry cases. Pour over egg mixture. Bake for 20–25 minutes
or until puffed and golden. Makes about 24.

Leek, Fetta and Sun-dried Tomato Quiches

Mini Lamb Shashlyh

2 tbsps olive oil
1 lemon finely grated and juiced
1 clove garlic, crushed
1 tsp dried oregano
salt and freshly ground black pepper
2.2 lb/1kg lamb backstrap, cut into 1 in/3cm cubes

Cucumber and Yoghurt Dipping Sauce
¾ cup natural yoghurt
⅓ cup finely diced Lebanese cucumber
2 tbsps lemon juice

Combine oil, lemon rind, lemon juice, garlic, oregano, salt and pepper
in a shallow ceramic dish. Add lamb, cover with plastic wrap and place
in the fridge to marinate for 2–3 hours. Cook lamb on a char-grill for
3–5 minutes or until cooked to your liking, turning from time to time.
Place on a serving plate and serve with toothpicks and dipping sauce.
Makes about 24.

Mini Lamb Shashlyh

Mini Chicken and Mushroom Pies

Mini Chicken and Mushroom Pies

olive oil spray
2 tbsps olive oil
14 oz/400g chicken mince
2 cloves garlic, crushed
5 oz/150g button mushrooms, finely chopped
2 shallots (green onions), thinly sliced
2 tbsps fresh thyme leaves
$\frac{1}{3}$ cup sour cream
salt and freshly ground black pepper
3 sheets shortcrust pastry, thawed
3 sheets puff pastry, thawed
1 egg, lightly beaten

Preheat oven to 430°C/220°C. Lightly grease 2 x 12 tart or patty cases, (2 in/6cm in diameter), with olive oil spray. Heat oil in a fry pan. Add chicken mince and cook for 3 minutes. Add garlic, mushrooms and shallots and cook for a further 3 minutes. Transfer to a bowl to cool. Stir in thyme leaves and sour cream, and season with salt and pepper. Cut shortcrust pastry and puff pastry into $2\frac{3}{4}$ in/7cm rounds. Line tart cases with shortcrust pastry. Divide chicken mixture evenly between tart cases. Lightly brush edges with water and place puff pastry rounds on top. Using a fork gently press edges together. Make a slit in the top and brush with beaten egg. Bake for 20 minutes or until puffed and golden. Makes about 24.

Beef and Sauerkraut Triangles

2 tbsps olive oil
½ brown onion, finely chopped
½ lb/250g beef mince
2½ oz/75g button mushrooms, finely chopped
½ cup sauerkraut
salt and freshly ground black pepper
2 tbsp butter, melted
8 sheets filo pastry

Preheat oven to 400°F/200°C. Line 2 baking trays with baking paper. Heat 1 tablespoon oil in a frying pan. Add onion and cook for 3 minutes or until soft. Add beef mince and cook for 2 minutes. Stir in mushrooms and cook for a further 2 minutes. Add sauerkraut, salt and pepper and stir well to combine. Transfer mixture to a bowl to cool. Combine remaining oil and butter in a bowl. Place 1 sheet fillo pastry on a clean work surface. Brush lightly with oil mixture. Top with another piece of filo pastry. Cut pastry crossways into 6 strips. Place tablespoons of mixture at one end of the pastry and fold over to form triangles. Brush ends and tops with oil mixture. Repeat with remaining pastry and beef mixture. Place triangles on prepared baking trays and bake for 20 minutes or until golden and crisp. Makes about 24.

Beef and Sauerkraut Triangles

Chicken Drumettes

Chicken Drumettes

¼ cup olive oil
¼ cup tomato sauce
2 tbsps honey
1 tbsp barbecue sauce
1 tbsp Dijon mustard
3 tsps Worcestershire sauce
2 cloves garlic, crushed
2.2 lb/1kg chicken drumettes

Combine olive oil, tomato sauce, honey, barbecue sauce, Dijon mustard, Worcestershire sauce and garlic in a shallow ceramic dish. Add chicken and coat well in mixture. Cover with plastic wrap and place in the fridge to marinate for 2–3 hours. Preheat oven to 400°F/ 200°C. Line a baking tray with foil. Place chicken on a rack over the baking tray. Bake in the oven for 30–35 minutes or until cooked. Makes about 18–20.

Notes

Notes

Notes

Notes

Index

Aberfoyle	14	Chi Chi	46	Greyhound	78
Absolut Wonder	14	Chicken Drumettes	123	Harvey Wallbanger	78
Appletini	14	Chocolate Raspberry Martini	46	Herb Blinis with Salmon Roe	105
Aqueduct	19	Chocolatini	46	Kamikaze	83
Badgertini	19	Citron Dragon	51	Kangaroo Cocktail	83
Bay Breeze	19	Clamato Cocktail	51	Karoff	83
Beef and Sauerkraut Triangles	120	Cosmopolitan	51	Leek, Fetta and Sun-dried Tomato Quiches	114
Beer Buster	22	Cranberry Christmas Punch	54	Long Island Iced Tea	86
Bewitched	22	Czarine	54	Marinated Stuffed Mushrooms	110
Black and Silver	22	Deanne	54	Mini Chicken and Mushroom Pies	119
Black Eye	27	Deliberation	59	Mini Lamb Shashlyh	116
Black Magic	27	Dessert Shield	59	Morning Glory	86
Black Russian	27	Dusty Dog	59	Moscow Mule	86
Blood Hound	30	Electric Lemonade	62	Pork Frickadellas	98
Bloody Mary	30	Electric Martini	62	Salami and Cheese Pumpernickel Squares	109
Bloody Mary Oyster Shots	101	Exterminator	62	Salty Dog	91
Blue Hawaii	35	Firefly	67	Sausage Crostini with Sauerkraut	102
Blue Lagoon	35	Flirtini	67	Screwdriver	91
Blue Martini	35	Flying Dutchman	67	Sex on the Beach	91
Blue Monday	38	Fools Gold	70	Smoked Fish and Egg Turnovers	113
Bluebeard	30	Fudgesicle	70	Smoked Salmon Canapés	106
Brass Monkey	38	Fuzzy Navel	70	Vodka Collins	94
Bullfrog	38	Gale at Sea	75	White Russian	94
Butterscotch Martini	43	Gibson	75		
Cape Cod	43	Godchild	75		
Cherry Ripe	43	Godmother	78